Deadly Democracy

The Election That Pushed America to the Brink

Eleanor T. Whitfield

Table of Contents

Introduction

The year 1872 was meant to represent a turning moment for America. The Civil War had finished, and President Ulysses S. Grant, the Union's hero, was fighting for re-election, anxious to realize the promise of Reconstruction—a multiracial democracy. But the promise of freedom and equality was under threat.

The South, reeling from defeat, was simmering with hatred, and white supremacist organizations like the Ku Klux Klan had emerged to attack newly emancipated Black residents. In Louisiana, the political landscape was a battleground, not of ideas, but of violence and carnage. As the election neared, the streets of New Orleans were scarlet with blood. Rival governors claimed power, crowds assaulted voters at voting booths, and an unusual sprint by train from New York to Louisiana became a physical war for control of a state.

At the center of this turbulence stands the Colfax Massacre—where at least 150 Black men were massacred by white militias—a chilling reminder of the depths to which foes of democracy will go to protect their power.

The Election of 1872 was more than simply a political contest—it was a war for the spirit of America. In *Deadly Democracy: The Election That Pushed America to the Brink*, we revisit this violent and tumultuous election to investigate how the promise of Reconstruction was destroyed, leaving behind a legacy of segregation and inequality that would persist for a century. This is the tale of a country that almost lost itself, and the lessons it offers for today's sharply divided political environment.

Chapter 1: The Aftermath of the Civil War

The conclusion of the American Civil War in 1865 was characterized by optimism and expectation. The country had experienced four years of violent struggle that resulted in more than 600,000 fatalities, and with the Union's triumph, the institution of slavery was finally abolished.

President Abraham Lincoln's Emancipation Proclamation created the framework for freedom, and with the approval of the 13th Amendment, slavery was effectively terminated throughout the nation. Yet, although the conflict was done, the larger fight for equality and togetherness was only starting. The

Reconstruction era, which followed the war, symbolized both the nation's greatest intentions and its worst failings, setting the stage for decades of racial struggle and injustice.

The Hopes and Failures of Reconstruction

Reconstruction was the period immediately after the Civil War (1865-1877), during which the federal government worked to reconstruct the South, integrate freed slaves into American society, and defend their newly earned rights.

Lincoln's vision for Reconstruction was one of leniency, hoping to heal the nation's wounds swiftly while expanding civil rights to African Americans. After his murder, however, the reins of Reconstruction were given to his successor, Andrew Johnson, whose attitude to reintegration was significantly more conciliatory toward the

Southern states, and less protective of Black rights.

The prospects of Reconstruction were first strong. The 13th Amendment ended slavery, while the 14th and 15th Amendments provided citizenship and vote to African Americans, marking the most substantial extension of civil rights in U.S. history. The Freedmen's Bureau formed in 1865, strove to give education, healthcare, and job help to millions of freed slaves, providing them a footing in their new lives.

Schools for African Americans blossomed, and for the first time, Black men held political office in the South, serving as congressmen, senators, and even state governors.

However, these improvements quickly faced intense resistance. Southern states, furious about federal intrusion and the loss of their traditional way of life, utilized all means possible to resist. President Johnson's indulgent policies toward the South enabled many former Confederates to recover political influence, but his vetoes of critical civil rights legislation galvanized Southern opposition.

Congress, headed by the more radical Republicans, wanted to enforce stronger Reconstruction policies by dividing the South into military districts, mandating states to accept the new amendments, and ensuring Black suffrage. Yet, the fissures based on Reconstruction were starting to appear.

Economic instability also affected the South during Reconstruction. The carnage of the Civil War had left Southern infrastructure in shambles, and the collapse of the plantation economy, without enslaved labor, decimated the region's riches.

The economic realities intensified racial tensions, as many impoverished whites struggled to adapt to the new labor system and competed with liberated African Americans for employment. The Southern economy's delayed recovery also fostered hostility against Reconstruction efforts.

The federal government's authority to enforce Reconstruction legislation was limited. Despite the presence of Union forces in the South, local governments and militias, frequently sympathetic to white supremacist groups, failed to protect Black civilians from violence and intimidation. Over time, the Northern people became sick of the frequent confrontations in the South, leading to a lack of political will to continue the costly and grueling process of Reconstruction.

The final defeat of Reconstruction occurred with the Compromise of 1877, which signaled the end of federal action in the South. In return for settling the disputed 1876 presidential election in favor of Republican Rutherford B. Hayes, federal soldiers were withdrawn, leaving African Americans in the South susceptible to the rise of white supremacy. The age of Reconstruction, once filled with optimism for racial equality, ended with the entrenchment of segregation and the establishment of Jim Crow laws, which would dominate Southern life for over a century.

Southern Resistance to Federal Authority

From the onset, Southern opposition to federal authority was a distinguishing aspect of Reconstruction. Former Confederate officials and their followers in the South were vehemently opposed to the Reconstruction measures enforced by the federal government, especially those that extended civil rights to African Americans.

For many white Southerners, Reconstruction was considered an assault on their way of life, one that upended the social order and humiliated the former Confederate states.

Southern resistance took numerous forms, both legal and extralegal. Politically, Southern governments worked to undermine Reconstruction by establishing a series of legislation known as "Black Codes," aimed to limit the liberties of African Americans. These rules differed from state to state but usually attempted to preserve a system of racial hierarchy and control.

Black Codes limited the sorts of employment that African Americans could take, restricted their travel, and aimed to reimpose circumstances comparable to slavery, such as compelling freedmen to sign annual work contracts or risk incarceration. The laws were a blatant effort to reverse the achievements won by the liberation of slavery and to retain white dominance in the post-war South.

White Southerners often used violence and intimidation to fight federal power. Paramilitary organizations, most memorably the Ku Klux Klan, formed throughout the South as a direct reaction to Reconstruction.

These organizations targeted African Americans, as well as white Republicans, Northerners (known as "carpetbaggers"), and Southern supporters of Reconstruction (called "scalawags"). Through a campaign of terror, they aimed to discourage African Americans from voting, holding office, or enjoying their newfound rights.

Resistance to Reconstruction was not restricted to violent fanatics. Southern state administrations, after they were readmitted to the

Union, tried to dismantle Reconstruction legislation by legal methods. Many Southern politicians created legislation that virtually negated federal safeguards for Black individuals, while friendly judges and law enforcement officials turned a blind eye to violence and prejudice.

This entrenched opposition guaranteed that even when the federal government implemented laws aimed to protect African Americans, local and state governments in the South undercut those efforts at every opportunity.

The Northern reaction to this opposition was varied. Initially, Radical Republicans in Congress pushed hard to impose Reconstruction, writing laws to protect African Americans and deploying federal soldiers to enforce them. But over time, Northern resolve faded. Economic worries, political scandals, and tiredness from years of fighting prompted North people to turn away from the South's woes. By the time of the Compromise of 1877, Southern opposition had essentially succeeded, and federal power in the South had all but evaporated.

The Birth of the Ku Klux Klan and White Supremacist Movements

The Ku Klux Klan (KKK), formed in 1865 by Confederate soldiers in Pulaski, Tennessee, rapidly became the most prominent emblem of Southern opposition to Reconstruction. While originally beginning as a social club, the Klan swiftly grew into a paramilitary organization with a sole mission: to restore white supremacy via murder and terror. The Klan's methods included lynching, whipping, arson, and murder, targeting Black individuals and their white sympathizers.

The Klan's development may be directly attributable to the hatred many Southern whites felt against the new social and political order created by Reconstruction. The enfranchisement of Black males and their involvement in Southern administrations was regarded as a direct challenge to the established power structure. The Klan intended to reverse these victories by scaring African Americans into submission, stopping them from voting, and targeting individuals who supported Reconstruction programs.

The federal government sought to curb the Klan's violence with legislation, particularly the Enforcement Acts of 1870 and 1871, which declared it a federal criminal to interfere with someone's right to vote and enabled the president to use military action to suppress Klan activities. These regulations were partly successful in reducing the Klan's power in the early 1870s.

Still, the advent of other white supremacist organizations, such as the White League and the Red Shirts, guaranteed that violent opposition remained. These organizations, like the Klan, employed terror methods to undermine Reconstruction and reestablish white rule in the South.

The Klan's presence started to decline following the government onslaught, but the philosophy it represented survived. White supremacist groups in the South continued to organize and expand, setting the framework for the ultimate construction of Jim Crow laws, which institutionalized racial segregation and disenfranchised Black Americans for centuries. The legacy of these movements would plague the South for decades, as the ideals of white supremacy were profoundly embedded in the region's political and social fabric.

Chapter 2: The Candidates and Their Platforms

Ulysses S. Grant, the triumphant Union commander turned president, entered the 1872 election seeking a second term. His administration was chiefly distinguished by his uncompromising devotion to Reconstruction, and the federal government's endeavor to reconstruct the South and incorporate newly liberated African Americans into the fabric of American democracy.

Grant was a firm defender of civil rights, especially for African Americans, and he thought that the federal government had a responsibility to preserve their rights in the face of violent resistance from the South.

Grant's administration had made some important progress in this area. The ratification of the 15th Amendment in 1870, which guaranteed African American males the right to vote, was a major victory.

Under Grant's command, federal soldiers were stationed in Southern states to enforce Reconstruction legislation and prevent violent uprisings by organizations like the Ku Klux Klan, which had arisen as a militant movement opposing Black suffrage and civil rights.

However, Grant's first tenure had not been without controversy. His presidency was beset by corruption scandals, most notably the Crédit Mobilier scam and the Whiskey Ring. While Grant himself was not personally involved, the idea of widespread wrongdoing tarnished his image. His detractors regarded him as a leader who had lost control of his government, surrounded by inept or dishonest advisers.

Despite these problems, Grant remained popular in the North, especially among Republicans who backed his Reconstruction efforts. His campaign highlighted the necessity to sustain federal engagement in the South to preserve the rights of newly freed slaves and maintain the fragile peace that had been secured at such a great cost.

Grant's platform was a defense of the accomplishments gained during Reconstruction and a pledge to safeguard the Union's success by ensuring that the South would not return to its old social order.

Grant's reelection campaign offered an image of a nation still mending from the traumas of the Civil War. He characterized the election as a choice between continuing the arduous work of Reconstruction or allowing the South to revert to the violent racial hierarchies that had caused the war. His message was clear: the federal government needed to continue the course to protect the Union's moral and political victories.

Horace Greeley: The Unlikely Liberal Reformer

Horace Greeley, Grant's adversary in the 1872 election, was an odd and unexpected candidate. A distinguished newspaper editor and publisher of the *New York Tribune*, Greeley was a man of contrasts. He had long been a champion for abolition and other progressive issues, but he found himself heading a coalition that included

Democrats, many of whom were former Confederates hostile to Reconstruction.

Greeley was nominated by the Liberal Republican Party, a party that had split away from the mainstream Republican Party. The Liberal Republicans were disillusioned with Grant's administration, notably its handling of Reconstruction and the corruption scandals that had marred the government's reputation. They feared that Grant's heavy-handed attitude to the South was doing more damage than good, inciting animosity and bloodshed rather than achieving peace.

For Greeley and his followers, the moment had come to move past the Civil War and concentrate on national unity. Their program advocated for a halt to federal military engagement in the South, claiming that Southern states should be permitted to run their affairs without Northern intrusion. This approach, known as "home rule," was popular in the South and among white Democrats, but it was a hard pill for African Americans and civil rights supporters to swallow.

Despite his credentials as an abolitionist, Greeley's campaign drew strong support from Democrats who saw in him a chance to demolish Reconstruction and reinstate white dominance in the South. Greeley's message of national unity, paired with his proposals for civil service reform and an end to political corruption, resonated with voters who were sick of the chaos and carnage that had followed the Civil War.

Yet, Greeley was not a sophisticated politician. He was widely considered as odd, with a reputation for unpredictable conduct and a propensity to alienate prospective allies. His choice to accept the Democratic candidacy, in addition to the Liberal Republican nomination, further hampered his campaign.

Many Republicans, notably African Americans and abolitionists, were perplexed by his collaboration with Democrats, especially those who had battled to protect slavery only a few years before.

Greeley's program also highlighted economic change, notably the need to handle the country's rising debt and the financial hardship created by wartime rebuilding operations. He argued for decreased tariffs and fiscal conservatism, appealing to those who thought that the federal government was spending too much on Reconstruction and the military occupation of the South. His commitment to "let the South alone" was meant to stimulate economic development by enabling Southern states to rebuild without federal involvement.

Despite his progressive credentials, Greeley's candidacy was hurt by his inability to unify the diverse groups backing him. While he attracted some Liberal Republicans and Democrats, his campaign lacked the wide popularity required to defeat a popular incumbent like Grant. Moreover, his involvement with Democrats, many of whom were antagonistic to civil rights, alienated his erstwhile supporters in the abolitionist movement.

The Political Climate: Corruption Accusations, Economic Pressures, and Reform Promises

The political situation in 1872 was riddled with tension and uncertainty. The country was still recuperating from the Civil War, and although Reconstruction had brought tremendous reforms, notably in the South, it had also caused profound divides.

The violent pushback against Reconstruction in the South, along with mounting fears about corruption in the federal government, made the 1872 election a combustible one.

Corruption was a serious concern on both sides. Grant's administration had been stained by scandals, prompting many to doubt his leadership and the integrity of his government.

Although Grant himself was never personally involved in these scandals, the impression of corruption was enough to drive the Liberal Republicans' breakaway movement and their desire for change. Greeley's supporters contended that Grant's government had grown complacent and corrupt and that fresh leadership was required to clean up Washington.

Economic forces also had a crucial effect in molding the political atmosphere. The country was suffering from debt from the Civil War, and there were rising worries about the cost of Reconstruction, notably the expenditure of retaining federal soldiers in the South.

Many Northern voters, especially in the business sector, were growing more anxious about the country's financial viability. Greeley's arguments for economic prudence and limited government expenditure resonated with many who thought that the federal government was overreaching in its attempts to transform the South.

At the same time, the subject of how to incorporate the South back into the Union remained controversial. Grant and the Radical Republicans thought that Reconstruction was necessary to preserve the rights of African Americans and prevent the South from returning to its prewar social order.

They contended that federal monitoring was vital to safeguard Black voters and officeholders from the violence and intimidation they experienced at the hands of white supremacists.

Greeley and the Liberal Republicans, on the other hand, thought that it was time for the federal government to pull aside and let the South rule itself. They believed that continuing military occupation and federal interference were simply stoking animosity and violence and that the best way to foster reconciliation was to restore "home rule" to Southern states.

This attitude appealed to many white Southerners and Northern Democrats who opposed Reconstruction and were eager to see federal soldiers evacuated from the South.

Ultimately, the 1872 election was about more than simply the candidates—it was a referendum on the destiny of the nation. The struggle between Grant and Greeley emphasized the wide differences that remained in postwar America. It was a war over the meaning of Reconstruction, the role of the federal government, and the future of civil rights.

For Grant and his allies, the election was about maintaining the hard-won accomplishments of the Civil War and ensuring that the nation would not backslide into the bloodshed and inequity of the past. For Greeley and his alliance, it was about going past the conflict and rebuilding the nation through reconciliation and reform.

Chapter 3: Louisiana: A Powder Keg

By 1872, Louisiana was the core of the post-Civil War fight for dominance in the South, when the political, racial, and social strains of Reconstruction clashed fiercely. Once a bulwark of the Confederacy, Louisiana was forced to face the drastic changes caused by the end of slavery and the unexpected political empowerment of emancipated Black individuals.

The Reconstruction Amendments—the 13th, 14th, and 15th—had abolished slavery, provided citizenship to African Americans, and allowed Black males the ability to vote. In theory, these amendments promised a new era of equality. In reality, they triggered a furious response from many white Southerners who refused to accept the new social order.

Louisiana became a significant battlefield for control over the post-war South. With a sizable Black population—many of whom had been slaves only a few years earlier—the state epitomized the promises and dangers of Reconstruction. In the towns and countryside alike, newly liberated Black men started engaging in politics, competing for office, and creating partnerships with Northern Republicans who wished to reconstruct the South and promote racial equality.

This growing political authority, however, was greeted with tremendous hostility. White landowners, former Confederate soldiers, and others who had prospered from the antebellum social system perceived the growth of Black political power as a direct threat to their way of life. The animosity among white Southerners rose as Black men took on important positions in municipal and state administration.

The spectacle of Black voters, lawmakers, and officeholders making choices for a state that had formerly kept them in bondage exacerbated the fury of many white individuals.

The fight for political influence between the races was not restricted to the voting box. Violence became a regular weapon used by white racists to discourage Black political engagement. Louisiana's racial tensions transformed its streets, farms, and towns into battlefields. This violent dynamic laid the setting for a tumultuous and deadly election season in

1872, one that would threaten the fundamental foundations of the state and the country.

Political Factions and Racial Violence: The Rise of Paramilitary Groups

As Reconstruction proceeded, Louisiana grew more split along racial and political lines. The Republican Party, which had championed the cause of freedom and civil rights for Black individuals, dominated the political landscape in the South, especially among newly enfranchised Black voters.

In contrast, the Democratic Party, mostly consisting of white Southerners and former Confederates, opposed Reconstruction and wanted to restore the state to white dominance.

Within this combustible milieu, paramilitary organizations like the White League and the Knights of the White Camelia arose. These groups were devoted to utilizing violence and intimidation to reestablish white supremacy in the South.

Unlike the Ku Klux Klan, which operated in secret, the White League was an overtly militant organization that engaged in coordinated, armed assaults against Black communities and Republican politicians. Their purpose was simple: to undo the victories of Reconstruction via intimidation and force.

The White League and kindred organizations utilized guerilla methods, ambushing Black individuals, Republican officeholders, and anybody who backed Reconstruction policies.

They deliberately targeted Black voters during elections, frequently with severe intimidation techniques at voting booths. The presence of armed white men outside polling booths became a familiar sight in Louisiana, effectively silencing Black voters who feared for their lives.

One of the most horrifying incidents of this racial violence happened in the lead-up to the 1872 election. In Colfax, Louisiana, a disagreement over the results of a municipal election evolved into an all-out murder.

Armed white supremacists, angry by the political power of the Black residents who had gained control of the local government, launched an assault on the Black community. Over many hours, they massacred more than 150 Black men, making the Colfax Massacre one of the bloodiest episodes of racial violence during Reconstruction. The tragedy acted as a message to Black individuals throughout Louisiana: political engagement may cost them their lives.

The development of paramilitary organizations in Louisiana was not a random phenomenon—it was a purposeful reaction to the perceived danger of Black political power. These gangs were well-organized, well-armed, and had the implicit backing of many white leaders and individuals who wanted to see Reconstruction fail. Through violence and intimidation, they succeeded in establishing an environment of dread and disorder that hampered the delicate progress of Reconstruction.

The Role of the Republican Party in the South's Shifting Political Landscape

During Reconstruction, the Republican Party in Louisiana and throughout the South was a combination of Northern "carpetbaggers," Southern white "scalawags," and newly enfranchised Black voters. Together, they sought to restore the Southern economy, promote civil rights, and establish a more inclusive political system.

In Louisiana, the Republican Party first achieved considerable success in developing a multiracial democracy. Black males were elected to municipal and state posts, and the state even sent its first Black representative, Joseph Rainey, to Congress.

However, the Republican Party's position in Louisiana was always fragile. Many white Southerners considered the Republicans as foreigners who had imposed a foreign set of beliefs on the South. The party's attempts to promote racial equality and create political chances for Black residents were greeted with resistance by white Democrats, who considered themselves the true rulers of Louisiana.

As tensions increased, the Republican Party found itself stuck in a deadly game. To keep control of the state, the party had to reconcile the demands of its Black followers with the violent opposition of white supremacists.

This was especially problematic in a state like Louisiana, where the Republican Party depended largely on federal backing to preserve order. President Ulysses S. Grant dispatched federal soldiers to the state many times to quash uprisings and safeguard Black inhabitants from paramilitary brutality.

The 1872 election constituted a turning point for the Republican Party in Louisiana. The state was bitterly split, and both Republican and Democratic groups claimed victory. The Republican candidate for governor, William Pitt Kellogg, and the Democratic candidate, John McEnery, both proclaimed themselves victors. The outcome was a political impasse that crippled the state administration and led to widespread rioting in the streets.

This unstable scenario was aggravated by the activities of the federal government. President Grant, reluctant to enable Democrats to destroy the Reconstruction administration, endorsed the Republican claim to power and deployed federal soldiers to impose Kellogg's governorship. This decision further enraged white Southerners, who regarded it as an illegal federal meddling in state matters.

The Republican Party's dependence on federal soldiers and its shaky grasp on power underlined the fragility of Reconstruction in Louisiana. While the party had succeeded in achieving legislative power for Black individuals and initiating reforms aimed at establishing a more equal society, it was continually under threat from violent white supremacist organizations and entrenched Southern elites.

The party's effort to keep authority would eventually end in defeat, as the forces of white supremacy proved too strong to resist without persistent federal assistance.

The aftermath of the 1872 election signaled the beginning of the end of Reconstruction in Louisiana. Over the following several years, white Democrats steadily recovered control of the state via a mixture of violence, voting suppression, and political manipulation.

By 1877, when federal soldiers were removed from the South, the Republican Party's experiment in multiracial democracy had crumbled. Louisiana, like most of the South, would be governed by white Democrats for decades to come, and the state would become a bulwark of Jim Crow laws and segregation.

In the years after the Civil War, Louisiana became a microcosm of the greater battles that characterized Reconstruction throughout the

South. The state's exploding racial and political tensions, the growth of dangerous paramilitary organizations, and the Republican Party's ambitions to construct a multiracial democracy all clashed in a brutal fight for power. The 1872 election was a key milestone in this conflict, demonstrating the fundamental differences that endangered the viability of American democracy.

Chapter 4: Voting Amid Violence

The Election of 1872 was no ordinary democratic event. Across the United States, especially in the South, voting became a risky act. For the first time since the Civil War, African Americans, who had been given the right to vote by the 15th Amendment, were exercising their political authority.

But the promise of democracy was greeted with furious and deadly resistance by white supremacist organizations, especially in areas like Louisiana, where tensions between racial and political factions had reached a boiling point.

Election day in 1872, particularly in the Deep South, was characterized by widespread dread and intimidation. While voting was supposed to be a simple civic obligation, it became a war for survival. White paramilitary groups, such as the Ku Klux Klan and the White League, tried to retain white rule by terror.

These organizations monitored voting centers, frequently armed, making it obvious that any Black man who dared to cast a ballot was putting his life in danger. The purpose wasn't only to tilt the election in favor of the Democrats, but to convey a larger message: Black political engagement would not be permitted.

In New Orleans, the core of Louisiana's political storm, election day was characterized as tense and dangerous. Armed militias patrolled the streets, and any effort by Black individuals to access voting locations was greeted with threats of violence. Many were violently beaten, and some were even murdered. The dread was obvious, not only among voters but among election officials, some of whom were involved in suppressing the Black vote.

Many polling stations were nothing more than scenes of open conflict between groups, with guns fired and violent fights breaking out in broad daylight.

This environment of intimidation and terror wasn't unique to Louisiana. Across the Southern states, African American voters faced comparable obstacles. Reports of crowds encircling voting booths, threats of lynching, and targeted assaults on Black community leaders were prevalent. The psychological toll was severe. For many, the option was simple: keep quiet or risk execution.

Widespread Voter Suppression and Fraud

The violence and intimidation were part of a bigger plan of voter suppression that marred the 1872 election. White Democrats, especially in the South, were desperate to recover political power lost during Reconstruction, and they utilized several techniques to suppress the Black vote. These varied from direct physical assault to more covert types of deception and deceit.

One of the most popular strategies was voter intimidation at voting booths. Armed white mobs would congregate around these areas, creating a dangerous atmosphere aimed to frighten off Black votes. In other situations, poll workers—often sympathetic to the Democratic cause—would simply refuse to let Black individuals vote. Even if a Black voter managed to reach the polling place, they would frequently encounter threats and intimidation inside, being informed that casting their vote would lead to reprisals against their family or communities.

Voter fraud was another major component of this suppression. Many polling locations reported inflated voter counts, with the names of dead or fraudulent persons added to the registers to enhance the Democratic vote total. In several situations, votes cast by Black voters were simply destroyed or substituted with fake ones supporting the white Democratic candidates. Election officials, particularly in regions controlled by white nationalists, were regularly engaged in this fraud, manipulating results or reporting figures that bore little similarity to the actual votes cast.

One especially known type of suppression was the "stuffing" of vote boxes. In areas with substantial Black populations, Democrats would bring in massive quantities of fake votes to ensure their win.

When the polls closed, the counting process was routinely skewed to favor white Democratic candidates, even when the actual votes indicated a clear preference for the Republican ticket, which at the time represented the party of Lincoln and Reconstruction. As a consequence, the official results in many locations were entirely at variance with the political reality on the ground.

These efforts were complemented by the legal manipulation of voter registration laws. In Louisiana and other Southern states, newly established legislation was meant to make it difficult for Black voters to register. Literacy exams, property restrictions, and other arbitrary criteria were used to prohibit huge numbers of Black individuals from voting.

These hurdles were selectively enforced, ensuring that white voters—many of whom could not satisfy the standards themselves—were permitted to vote while Black individuals were turned away.

The scale of voter suppression during the 1872 election was astonishing. In certain locations, Black voter participation was cut by as much as 50% compared to prior elections. This artificial restriction of the vote ensured that white Democrats recovered control of many municipal and state governments, thereby nullifying the political victories earned by Black residents during the early years of Reconstruction.

First-Hand Accounts of the Chaos at the Polls

The violence and intimidation that marked the 1872 election are described in the tragic first-hand recollections of individuals who experienced the mayhem. These tales give a vivid and distressing view into the realities of voting in a society still coping with the legacy of slavery and civil war.

One account from a Black voter in Louisiana described the terror he faced as he approached the polling station: "I saw the white men gathered with their guns and clubs, and I knew they were waiting for us. They told me to go home, and that if I voted, I would not see my family again. I feared for my life, but I feared more for the future of my people if we did not stand our ground."

Another witness, a Republican election official in New Orleans, recalled the bedlam inside the polling station: "It was as if the war had come to our doorstep. Men were yelling, shoving, and fighting. The ballots were being torn apart, and anyone who dared speak in support of the Republican candidates was quickly silenced, either by threats or by blows."

In Colfax, Louisiana, the scene of one of the most severe incidents of election-related violence, a Black voter described the horrors of the Colfax Massacre. "We went to the polls, hoping our voices would be heard. But instead, they arrived with their weapons and torches. They encircled us, and there was no escape. We were defenseless and outnumbered, and they butchered us as if we were animals."

These reports were not isolated. Throughout the South, similar accounts surfaced, each more cruel than the last. In several cases, Black voters sought to hold their ground, resolute to exercise their right to vote despite the threats. Some got to cast their votes, but many more were turned away or assaulted before they could do so.

The violence at the polls was not restricted to voters. In other locations, Black election officials were targeted for assassination. In the days preceding the election, many prominent Black politicians and community leaders were slain or maimed in assaults meant to damage the Republican ticket and instill fear among Black voters. One such person was State Senator P.B.S. Pinchback, who barely evaded an assassination attempt in New Orleans. His survival became a rallying cry for Black voters, but the harm was done—many were too terrified to risk their lives for the vote.

For many Black voters, the election of 1872 was a harsh reminder that the promises of freedom and equality promised by Reconstruction were fragile and easily crushed. Despite the fortitude displayed by many, the violence and repression of that election laid the groundwork for the ultimate breakdown of Reconstruction and the emergence of Jim Crow laws, which would disenfranchise Black voters for centuries.

Chapter 5: The Battle for Louisiana

The 1872 election in Louisiana was a watershed for the nation's post-Civil War political and racial tensions. As the state recovered from the destruction of war, its future rested on Reconstruction efforts that attempted to build a multiracial democracy. Yet, opposition to these measures, backed by white supremacists and conservative Democrats, produced a combustible climate.

The election became the most notorious of its day, ending in a constitutional crisis, a violent fight for control, and a direct intervention by federal troops.

The Disputed Results in Louisiana and the Rise of Two Rival Governors

In 1872, Louisiana was one of the most highly fought battlegrounds of the Reconstruction era. Republicans, who had seized control of the state following the Civil War, were devoted to ensuring civil rights and political authority for Black inhabitants. Democrats, mostly consisting of former Confederates and white nationalists, were desperate to reclaim authority and re-establish white rule.

As the election results started coming in, it became evident that the outcome was far from resolved. Both the Republican and Democratic parties claimed victory in the contest for governor. Republican candidate William Pitt Kellogg, a fervent proponent of civil rights and government action in the South, proclaimed himself the winner. Meanwhile, Democratic candidate John McEnery, supported by white nationalist organizations, also gained the governorship. Each group accused the other of voting fraud, ballot stuffing, and corruption. Violence at polling sites, voter intimidation by paramilitary organizations like the White League, and major irregularities led to a chaotic election process.

The disputed results plunged the state into disarray. Each side set up its government, with McEnery forming a competing administration in opposition to Kellogg's. The issue was further compounded by Louisiana's existing racial tensions, which had previously sparked deadly battles between white militias and Black voters. McEnery's followers formed mostly of former Confederates and white racists, opposed the validity of Reconstruction and tried to undo the political achievements won by African Americans since the conclusion of the Civil War.

The upshot was two opposing administrations, each claiming legitimacy, and a state on the verge of civil war. Kellogg, recognized by President Ulysses S. Grant and the federal government, retained authority in name but had little jurisdiction outside of New Orleans.

McEnery, who had the support of many of the white populace, particularly in rural regions, was prepared to oppose the federal government's authority and capture the governorship by force if necessary. This power battle laid the setting for one of the most spectacular periods in American political history.

The Train Race to New Orleans: A Frantic Contest for Control of the State Government

As tensions increased, the struggle for control of Louisiana's state government became a race against time. The two warring groups, understanding that control of New Orleans meant control of the state, started a furious fight to take the city and its administrative infrastructure. In one of the most dramatic periods of the crisis, Republican and Democratic leaders launched rival efforts to visit New Orleans and physically take the state government's buildings.

Kellogg's Republican administration, reinforced by federal soldiers stationed in New Orleans, needed to safeguard the city as the seat of its government. At the same time, McEnery's Democrats, backed by well-armed militias and the White League, intended to capture the city by force. They felt that if they could dominate New Orleans, they could install McEnery as governor and remove the Republicans from office.

What ensued was a spectacular race, one that would come to embody the lawlessness and desperation of the moment. In January 1873, only days after the disputed election results, McEnery's followers seized a train from New York, seeking to reach New Orleans as swiftly as possible and take over the state government by any means necessary.

The train was filled with attorneys, politicians, and militiamen loyal to McEnery. This effort was part of a bigger plot to take the reins of power before the federal government could interfere.

However, Kellogg's allies caught wind of the scheme and immediately collected their troops to prevent McEnery's men from reaching the city. With the backing of federal forces stationed nearby, they were able to seize important government facilities, including the state capital, before McEnery's side arrived. Nevertheless, the atmosphere was electric with tension, and both sides readied for a violent conflict.

The spectacular rail race to New Orleans became a symbol of the total disarray of the 1872 election. It emphasized the desire of the Democrats to reclaim control of Louisiana and the shaky grip the Republicans held over a state sharply split by race and politics. While

McEnery's soldiers eventually failed to conquer New Orleans, the scene was prepared for additional bloodshed, as the dual administrations continued to strive for legitimacy.

The Federal Government's Response: The Military's Role in the Crisis

The prolonged issue in Louisiana garnered national attention, with the federal government obliged to determine how to manage the mounting possibility of violence and the constitutional problem of two conflicting governors.

President Ulysses S. Grant, a staunch backer of Reconstruction, had a tough issue. On one side, he sought to fulfill the federal government's commitment to Reconstruction and defend the rights of newly emancipated Black individuals.

On the other, he was leery of engaging too much in state matters, especially in the face of vehement Southern resistance and rising political opposition from Democrats in the North.

Grant's government finally concluded that the best way to end the problem was by the direct deployment of military force. Federal forces, already stationed in New Orleans, were instructed to guarantee that Kellogg's Republican administration stayed in power. This was a very contentious decision since it looked to some that the federal government was forcing its will on a Southern state by force, an act that many white Southerners considered an insult to their sovereignty.

The military played a significant role in avoiding an open civil war in Louisiana. Federal forces were dispatched to safeguard Kellogg's government and to keep order in the streets of New Orleans, which had become a hotspot for unrest.

In one memorable episode, federal troops intervened to disperse a gathering of McEnery's followers who had assembled at the state capital to take control. Their presence also helped to dampen the operations of the White League, a paramilitary organization that had committed acts of terrorism and intimidation to suppress Black voting and threaten Republican power.

Despite the military's presence, the situation remained tense. The Kellogg government's dependence on federal soldiers made it look weak and illegitimate in the view of many Louisianans, particularly white Democrats who regarded federal action as a continuation of Northern tyranny. For months, tensions simmered just below the surface, with violence breaking out occasionally around the state. Armed skirmishes between McEnery's followers and federal soldiers occurred occasionally, reinforcing the atmosphere of insecurity.

The federal government's participation in Louisiana culminated in a judicial struggle that would alter the direction of American history. In 1875, the U.S. Supreme Court took up the issue of *United States v. Cruikshank*, which stemmed from the Colfax Massacre, a horrific assault on Black Americans by white nationalists. The Court's verdict in favor of the white defendants substantially undermined the federal government's capacity to enforce civil rights legislation in the South, signifying the beginning of the end of Reconstruction.

As a consequence of the Supreme Court's verdict and rising Northern ambivalence for Reconstruction, federal soldiers were finally evacuated from Louisiana and other Southern states. This signified the breakdown of Reconstruction and the beginning of a new period of white supremacy and segregation in the South, one that would persist for almost a century.

Chapter 6: The Colfax Massacre

The Colfax Massacre of 1873 remains one of the most horrifying moments in American history, signifying the brutal end of Reconstruction's promise to build a multiracial democracy. Set in Colfax, Louisiana, the massacre saw white supremacists mercilessly slaughter over 150 Black men, many of them freedmen seeking to exercise their newly acquired rights as citizens.

This horrible tragedy became not merely a symbol of the post-Civil War South's violent resistance to Reconstruction, but also a key moment in America's retreat from the promise of equality for all.

The Brutal Attack in Colfax, Louisiana

By the early 1870s, the state of Louisiana was a hotbed of racial and political turmoil. Following the Civil War and the ratification of the 13th, 14th, and 15th Amendments, African Americans in the South started to acquire political influence. Many Black males were elected to government, particularly in towns like Colfax, where the main population was African American.

The town became a hotspot in the conflict between the newly enfranchised Black inhabitants and white Democrats trying to preserve control of state and municipal administrations. In the contentious gubernatorial election of 1872, the tension between the Republican and Democratic parties reached a breaking point. Both parties claimed victory, resulting in two parallel administrations in Louisiana. The political turbulence fueled racial animosities, and Colfax, situated in Grant Parish, became the hub of the battle.

When Republicans, who were overwhelmingly backed by Black people, seized possession of the Colfax courthouse to stake their claim to local governance, white Democrats and their armed paramilitary organizations were eager to take it back.

A paramilitary group known as the White League—a predecessor to groups like the Ku Klux Klan—formed to drive away the Republicans by force. On Easter Sunday, April 13, 1873, the white nationalist militia assembled, heavily armed, and marched on the courthouse.

The gathering of Black men, many of them veterans of the Union Army, had sought sanctuary inside the courtroom to preserve their political rights and oppose the approaching bloodshed. As the white crowd advanced, the defenders, ill-prepared and outnumbered, made a desperate stand. But they were no match for the White League's greater numbers and firepower.

After hours of intermittent shooting, the white assailants set the courthouse on fire, forcing the Black defenders to retreat into the surrounding countryside. As the men sought to flee, they were chased down and killed—some shot as they fled, others seized and slaughtered in cold blood. By the end of the day, more than 150 Black men were dead, and their remains were left scattered throughout the terrain.

The massacre was not an isolated act of violence but a calculated strike aimed to destroy Black political leadership. In the days immediately up to the massacre, local white leaders had publicly discussed preparations to seize the courtroom by any means necessary. The methodical nature of the assault indicated not only a desire for political control but also a deep-seated contempt for the principle of racial equality.

The Immediate Fallout: National Shock and Local Apathy

News of the tragedy circulated swiftly throughout the country, generating anger in some parts and apathy in others. Newspapers in the North criticized the violence, branding the slaughter as an outrage. The Republican-controlled federal government, still focused on implementing Reconstruction, voiced worry about the rising lawlessness in the South. Radical Republicans, who had been the architects of Reconstruction, regarded the Colfax Massacre as a sad indication that white Southern Democrats were prepared to use murder to keep Black Americans from obtaining full citizenship.

However, in the South, the attitude was dramatically different. Local authorities did nothing to investigate the atrocity, and little attempt was made to apprehend or punish the murderers.

The white supremacists responsible for the deaths were regarded as heroes in certain Southern communities, and the massacre was portrayed as a necessary act of self-defense against a claimed Black rebellion. The local press and public opinion in Louisiana sometimes minimized the violence or blamed the victims themselves, framing the murder as a sad but legitimate reaction to Republican "misrule."

The complacency of local leaders mirrored a wider problem: Reconstruction's underpinnings were collapsing. Although federal forces were still stationed in sections of the South to keep order, they were increasingly helpless to halt the widespread racial violence that followed the political conflicts. The Colfax Massacre became indicative of the federal government's incapacity to protect Black residents in the face of massive white opposition.

One of the most stunning features of the aftermath was the judicial reaction. Federal officials sought to bring the offenders to justice by prosecuting them under the Enforcement

Acts, laws aimed to repress the Ku Klux Klan and other white supremacist organizations. However, the subsequent case—*United States v. Cruikshank*—dealt a serious blow to the federal government's capacity to pursue racial violence.

How Colfax Became a Symbol of Reconstruction's Failure

The Colfax Massacre became a devastating emblem of the failure of Reconstruction, not simply because of the severity of the bloodshed, but also because of the judicial precedent that followed. In 1876, the U.S. Supreme Court handed its judgment in 'United States v. Cruikshank', declaring that the federal government had no power to prosecute people for breaches of the civil rights of Black Americans under the Enforcement Acts. The court argued that the 14th Amendment only extended to governmental activities, not individual acts of violence. In effect, the judgment put Black residents at the mercy of state governments, many of which were ruled by white supremacists.

The verdict in 'Cruikshank' significantly undermined the federal government's capacity to enforce civil rights legislation in the South, and it signaled the beginning of the end of Reconstruction.

Southern governments, emboldened by the judgment, escalated their attempts to disenfranchise Black voters and enforce racial segregation via Jim Crow legislation. The Supreme Court's ruling communicated to the country that the federal government would no longer interfere to safeguard the rights of Black Americans, allowing white supremacist organizations full reign to employ violence and intimidation to preserve their rule.

The legacy of the Colfax Massacre and *United States v. Cruikshank* was felt for decades. The killing itself was a striking indication of how deeply embedded racism and white supremacy were in Southern culture, but the legal and political implications were far more significant.

The federal government's pullback from protecting civil rights successfully permitted white Southerners to take back the gains achieved during Reconstruction, resulting in almost a century of racial segregation, disenfranchisement, and bloodshed.

In time, the Colfax Massacre slipped from public consciousness, eclipsed by other events in the Reconstruction period and the emerging narrative of the "Lost Cause," which idealized the Confederacy and minimized the horrors of racial murder in the South.

Yet, for many who study the history, Colfax remains one of the clearest illustrations of how Reconstruction failed—not because the principles of equality and democracy were faulty, but because they were brutally challenged by people determined to retain white dominance.

Chapter 7: Two Governors, One State

In the aftermath of the 1872 election, Louisiana became the core of a political crisis that drove the state to the verge of civil war. The election results were so vehemently disputed that, for a short but deadly time, Louisiana had two men claiming the position of governor—both supported by separate political groups, each accusing the other of fraud, and each eager to cling on to power by any means necessary.

This dual leadership pushed the state into violent instability, with publications throwing fuel to the flames and murder plots boiling the streets.

The Dual Governorship of Louisiana: The Violent Power Struggle

The beginnings of Louisiana's dual governorship arose from the wider national election in 1872, which put incumbent President Ulysses S. Grant against newspaper writer Horace Greeley. Although Grant won the national contest, the election in Louisiana was far more acrimonious, marred by voting intimidation, fraud, and bloodshed.

Both parties—the Republicans, who were loyal to Reconstruction, and the Democrats, who intended to reestablish white supremacy in the South—claimed triumph. The Republican candidate, William Pitt Kellogg, was proclaimed the winner by the state's Republican-controlled Returning Board. Kellogg supported the pro-Grant, pro-Reconstruction group and had the backing of many Black voters, who regarded him as a guardian of their newly earned rights. On the other side, John McEnery, the Democratic candidate, proclaimed himself the real governor, saying the election had been stolen by fraud and federal meddling. McEnery's agenda attempted to reverse Reconstruction measures, restrict Black political influence, and restore white control.

What ensued was an unprecedented power battle. Both Kellogg and McEnery established parallel governments, each claiming legitimacy. McEnery's followers, many of whom were former Confederates and members of white supremacist organizations like the White League, came to the streets in violent clashes with Kellogg's supporters, who were mostly

Black residents and pro-Reconstruction Republicans.

In New Orleans, McEnery and his supporters attacked the state capital, violently pushing Kellogg's elected legislature out of the building and installing McEnery as governor. For a little while, McEnery held the seat of government. However, Kellogg, backed by the federal government, refused to compromise. President Grant deployed federal forces to back Kellogg's claim, and the U.S. military forcefully removed McEnery from the statehouse, reinstalling Kellogg as governor.

But the violence didn't stop there. McEnery's followers refused to recognize Kellogg's authority, and armed gangs battled in the streets. The White League, a paramilitary force affiliated with McEnery, openly waged war against Kellogg's administration and Black residents, targeting Republican strongholds and launching deadly raids. By the end of 1873, Louisiana was a state under siege, with two administrations contending for power, and carnage a continuous reality.

The Role of Newspapers in Inflaming the Conflict

As the political war between Kellogg and McEnery developed, newspapers were important instruments for both sides, not just reporting the events but actively affecting public opinion. In the years after the Civil War, newspapers in Louisiana—and throughout the South—were intensely politicized. Rather than functioning as neutral sources of information, they were frequently extensions of political groups, boosting their respective causes and inflaming tensions.

Pro-McEnery publications, such *The New Orleans Times* and *The Daily Picayune*, depicted Kellogg and his followers as corrupt and despotic. They depicted the federal government's backing of Kellogg as an illegitimate occupation by northern soldiers and a continuation of the "oppression" the South had undergone during the Civil War.

These journals utilized aggressive language to stir outrage among white inhabitants, depicting Reconstruction as a direct danger to their way of life. Articles typically depicted Black residents as unsuited for political involvement, using racial rhetoric to justify voter suppression and violent opposition.

On the other side, pro-Kellogg periodicals, especially *The New Orleans Republican*, upheld the legality of Kellogg's administration and Reconstruction. These publications emphasized the violence and intimidation methods employed by McEnery's supporters, notably the White League, and urged for the federal government to intervene more aggressively to safeguard the rights of Black voters and elected officials. However, these pleas were frequently buried by the louder and more inflammatory language of the pro-McEnery press.

The press also had a significant role in creating the bigger story of the crisis. National journalists, especially in the North, interpreted the war in Louisiana as a reflection of the greater struggle over Reconstruction. Northern journalists were generally sympathetic to Kellogg, regarding him as a supporter of Black rights and a bulwark against the return of Confederate authority. Southern media, however, presented McEnery as a hero battling against federal expansion and tyranny.

As media on both sides of the argument pushed their versions of the facts, the gaps between McEnery's and Kellogg's followers widened, and the violence increased. What may have been a political argument became a full-blown social and racial struggle, with media openly promoting the opposition and violence that had already engulfed the state.

Assassination Plots and Street Battles: A State Teetering on the Edge of Civil War

The violent power struggle in Louisiana wasn't restricted to political posturing or verbal contests in the press. It spilled into the streets with deadly repercussions, as armed militias, murder plots, and brutal street skirmishes drove the state to the verge of civil war.

One of the most disturbing features of the dual governorship was the open talk of murders as a solution to settle the political situation. In a place where law and order had broken down, McEnery's followers regularly resorted to violence and threats of murder to attain their aims.

Attempts on the lives of Kellogg and his supporters were widespread. In New Orleans and around the state, Republican politicians, especially Black leaders, were often targeted for death by white supremacist militias. The threat of political violence was prevalent, and the collapse of faith in democratic procedures became irrevocable.

Meanwhile, McEnery's White League increased its campaign of intimidation. Modeled after the Ku Klux Klan, the White League was a paramilitary group that operated openly, targeting Black neighborhoods, scaring voters, and engaging in violent clashes with Kellogg's men. The group's purpose was simple: to frighten Black people and Republican sympathizers into obedience, ultimately undoing the gains accomplished during Reconstruction.

In one of the most notable episodes of this time, the Battle of Liberty Place, a full-scale conflict occurred in the streets of New Orleans. On

September 14, 1874, the White League launched a concerted attack on the city, battling with Kellogg's state militia and federal forces. For many days, New Orleans was a battle zone. The White League's fighters grabbed important government facilities and temporarily gained control of the city, forcing Kellogg to escape.

It was only until President Grant dispatched federal soldiers to reclaim the city that Kellogg's administration was restored. The bloodshed left scores dead, and the conflict became a symbol of the lawlessness and savagery that characterized Louisiana at this period.

The continual danger of murder and the regularity of street clashes highlighted how unstable Louisiana's democratic system had become. The state was no longer ruled by the rule of law but by the threat of violence. The 1872 election had fragmented Louisiana's society, and the legitimacy of the government—whether governed by McEnery or Kellogg—was continually in doubt.

As the violence increased, the rest of the nation watched in terror. Louisiana has become a case study in the hazards of disputed elections, political corruption, and racial violence. The federal government, which had long been devoted to safeguarding Reconstruction, started to reconsider its position in the South.

By the end of the 1870s, federal assistance in Louisiana would come to an end, and Reconstruction would fail, giving birth to the Jim Crow period that would rule the South for decades.

Chapter 8: The Legal Battle that Ended Reconstruction

The conclusion of the Civil War in 1865 generated optimism for a new age of equality and justice in the United States. With the ratification of the 13th, 14th, and 15th Amendments, the groundwork was established for a multiracial democracy where all people, regardless of race, would enjoy equal protection under the law.

However, this vision was vigorously disputed by Southern governments, who rejected Reconstruction efforts and wanted to reinstate white supremacy. The violent election of 1872 in Louisiana was a turning point, but it was the legal fight that followed—culminating in the notorious *United States v. Cruikshank* Supreme Court verdict in 1876—that eventually ended Reconstruction and prepared the way for the emergence of Jim Crow laws. This ruling had severe and far-reaching repercussions for civil rights in the U.S., leading to almost a century of segregation and disenfranchisement for Black Americans.

The Supreme Court Steps In The Infamous *United States v. Cruikshank* Ruling

At the center of the judicial dispute that ended Reconstruction was the *United States v. Cruikshank* lawsuit, which emerged from the tragic events of the Colfax Massacre in 1873. Following the fiercely fought governor election in Louisiana in 1872, tensions between white Democrats and Black Republicans in Colfax, a tiny town in Grant Parish, reached a tragic climax. White paramilitary gangs, aiming to gain political authority from the Black majority, assaulted and massacred over 150 Black males, most of whom had surrendered or were unarmed. The slaughter was typical of the violent opposition to Reconstruction in the South.

In the aftermath, federal prosecutors worked to bring justice to the victims of the slaughter. They indicted some of the white assailants under the Enforcement Acts of 1870, which had been created by Congress to safeguard the civil rights of Black residents, including their ability to vote, and to resist the development of the Ku Klux Klan. These statutes were created to enable federal authorities to intervene in situations where states failed to protect individuals from racial violence.

One of the primary acts cited in the case was the Enforcement Act of 1870, which made it a federal criminal to plot to deprive someone of their constitutional rights. Among the defendants in the Colfax case was William Cruikshank, who was accused of breaching the civil rights of the Black victims.

The federal government maintained that by engaging in the slaughter, Cruikshank and others had plotted to deprive the victims of their freedom to freely assemble and their right to vote—rights guaranteed by the Constitution and protected by the 14th and 15th Amendments.

However, the case did not result in a win for justice. The defendants appealed, and the case finally reached the U.S. Supreme Court in 1876. In a remarkable and heartbreaking judgment, the Court decided in favor of Cruikshank, overturning the convictions.

The opinion, given by Chief Justice Morrison Waite, represented a major turning point in American legal history and inflicted serious damage to the federal government's capacity to enforce civil rights legislation during Reconstruction.

The Court's rationale was predicated on a restrictive construction of the Constitution. It found that the 14th Amendment only extended to activities committed by state governments, not private persons. This meant that, although state governments could not violate people's constitutional rights, individuals or groups—such as the white paramilitary forces responsible for the Colfax Massacre—could not be punished by the federal government for violating the rights of Black residents.

In essence, the Court concluded that defending civil rights was the duty of the states, not the federal government unless state actors were directly engaged.

This ruling fundamentally undermined the Enforcement Acts and significantly curtailed the authority of the federal government to protect Black individuals from violence and intimidation. The Court also concluded that the freedom to assemble and the right to carry weapons were not provided by the federal

Constitution but existed only insofar as they were safeguarded by the state governments. The Cruikshank ruling left Black individuals in the South open to violent repression, since many Southern governments were either hesitant or involved in the operations of white supremacist organizations.

How the Court's Decision Paved the Way for Jim Crow Laws and Segregation

The United States v. Cruikshank verdict had immediate and far-reaching implications. By leaving the burden of defending civil rights entirely in the hands of the states—many of which were ruled by white supremacist governments—the decision cleared the path for the systematic disenfranchisement and segregation of Black persons. Southern governments took advantage of the verdict to implement a series of laws and policies aimed at robbing Black residents of their rights, notably their ability to vote.

Within a few years following the *Cruikshank* verdict, Southern states started passing what would come to be known as Jim Crow legislation. These regulations provided a legal basis for racial segregation in all sectors of public life, including schools, transportation, housing, and public amenities.

Poll levies, literacy tests, and grandfather clauses were adopted to disenfranchise Black voters, while white vigilante violence, frequently carried out with the implicit backing of state officials, continued to frighten and crush Black communities.

The Cruikshank judgment also laid the groundwork for later Supreme Court opinions that progressively eroded the civil rights of Black Americans. In The Civil Rights Cases of 1883, the Court knocked down the Civil Rights Act of 1875, which had barred racial discrimination in public accommodations, by declaring that Congress did not have the jurisdiction to control private acts of discrimination.

Then, in 1896, the Court's decision in Plessy v. Ferguson codified the notion of "separate but equal," solidifying racial segregation as the law of the country for decades to come.

The Cruikshank judgment was therefore a critical milestone in the unraveling of Reconstruction. By robbing the federal government of its jurisdiction to defend the civil rights of Black residents and leaving that obligation in the hands of unfriendly state governments, the decision facilitated the establishment of a racially divided society in the South. It also represented the federal government's retreat from the promises of Reconstruction and the abandoning of Black Americans to the mercy of unfriendly local authorities.

The Long-Term Impact on Civil Rights in the U.S.

The long-term significance of the United States v. Cruikshank verdict on civil rights in the U.S. cannot be emphasized. It essentially signaled the end of Reconstruction and the beginning of a lengthy period of racial segregation, disenfranchisement, and brutality against Black

Americans. For over a century following the verdict, Southern states maintained a severe system of racial segregation, enforced by law and by extralegal violence. The safeguards provided by the 14th and 15th Amendments were mostly meaningless since Black individuals were systematically barred from political and economic life.

The repercussions of the Cruikshank ruling were felt far into the 20th century. It wasn't until the Civil Rights Movement of the 1950s and 1960s that the federal government started to seriously confront the system of segregation and disenfranchisement that had been created in the aftermath of the verdict. Landmark laws like the Civil Rights Act of 1964 and the Voting Rights Act of 1965 were essential to erase the legal framework of Jim Crow that had been constructed in part due to the Supreme Court's ruling in Cruikshank.

The United States v. Cruikshank ruling also left a worrisome legacy in terms of the interplay between federal and state authority. By stating that the preservation of civil rights was largely a state obligation, the verdict permitted state governments to ignore federal authority when it came to questions of racial equality. This struggle between state and federal jurisdiction over civil rights would continue to define American politics and law for decades.

Chapter 9: The Election of 1872 and Its National Consequences

The Election of 1872 was one of the most contentious and tumultuous in American history, conducted during the difficult Reconstruction era that followed the Civil War. While Ulysses S. Grant gained a second term as President, the national repercussions of this election stretched well beyond a mere electoral win.

The 1872 election showed the fundamental differences inside the nation, not only between North and South but also among political groups. The immediate impact echoed throughout the country, leading to a crisis of democracy, the breakdown of Reconstruction, and the development of the "Solid South," where white Democrats reclaimed and kept power for decades.

A Crisis of Democracy

The Election of 1872 happened at a period when the United States was attempting to redefine itself in the wake of the Civil War. The war had technically abolished slavery, but the subject of how to integrate millions of freshly liberated African Americans into the political and social fabric of the country remained difficult.

The Republican Party, which had led the Union to victory, was in power, and Reconstruction programs attempted to expand civil rights and political involvement to previously enslaved Black Americans. However, this initiative encountered significant opposition, notably in the Southern states.

As election day neared, the 1872 campaign was characterized by charges of corruption, fraud, and massive voter intimidation, especially in Southern states like Louisiana. President Grant's administration was accused of cronyism, and his opponents, headed by Liberal Republican nominee Horace Greeley, gathered under the cry of political reform. This schism among the Republican Party broke its cohesiveness and prepared the setting for a fiercely disputed election.

In the South, where Reconstruction efforts were being faced with violent opposition from white supremacist organizations like the Ku Klux Klan, the 1872 election descended into actual conflict. Black voters, many of whom were casting their votes for the first time, suffered violent intimidation and suppression techniques. Armed militias and paramilitary organizations aimed to prevent Black residents from exercising their rights, and deadly conflicts occurred at voting booths. The Colfax Massacre, in which over 150 Black men were massacred by white militias, was one of the worst incidents of this brutality.

The political anarchy reached a height in Louisiana, where two alternative administrations claimed legitimacy, each supported by separate groups. This dual governorship—one Republican, the other Democratic—threw the state into additional chaos and functioned as a microcosm of the national situation. The federal government's incapacity to settle this conflict promptly or effectively mirrored the greater fragility of American democracy at the time. The events in Louisiana, along with comparable incidents of election violence and fraud throughout the South, showed the profound fractures in the democratic process, as parties eager to use violence and intimidation found themselves increasingly unrestrained by federal authority.

The crisis of democracy that emerged in the Election of 1872 signaled a greater national retreat from the ideals of Reconstruction. Despite Grant's re-election, the commitment to upholding civil rights and fair elections in the South was gradually fading. This degradation of democratic norms and the federal government's failure to face the violent suppression of Black voters prepared the ground for a larger breakdown of Reconstruction itself.

The End of Reconstruction: The Federal Government Abandons the South

The larger national consequences of the 1872 election included the eventual abandoning of Reconstruction by the federal government. Reconstruction had been a daring experiment aimed at changing the South, extending civil rights to African Americans, and bringing the area back into the Union on the ideals of equality.

However, the 1872 election proved that federal enforcement of these aims was increasingly impossible, particularly in the face of violent resistance from Southern whites.

Ulysses S. Grant's government had first taken a tough position against the bloodshed in the South. Grant dispatched federal soldiers to preserve order and assist Reconstruction administrations in Southern states. However, as his administration drew on, the political will to maintain these initiatives started to weaken.

Scandals within Grant's administration, combined with economic constraints from the Panic of 1873, drew national attention away from the South and onto other important issues. Northern voters, sick of the prolonged military presence in the South and the expense of Reconstruction, started to adjust their priorities.

The 1872 election represented a turning point in this retreat. While Grant won a convincing win against Greeley, it was evident that the

Republican Party's support for forceful Reconstruction programs was eroding. Many Republicans, particularly in the North, thought that Reconstruction had run its course and that it was time for the South to rule itself. This change in public attitude led to a slow weakening of federal control in Southern states, where white Democrats were already rallying to recover power.

The federal government's retreat from Reconstruction was not instantaneous, but the election of 1872 established the seeds for its ultimate failure. By the time of the Compromise of 1877, which essentially ended Reconstruction by removing federal soldiers from the South, the ideals of Reconstruction had been badly eroded. The federal government's abdication of its commitment to defending the rights of Black residents in the South enabled white supremacists to reclaim power, signifying the end of the short post-Civil War experiment in multiracial democracy.

The Rise of the Solid South: The Political Dominance of White Democrats for Decades

As federal backing for Reconstruction diminished, Southern states swiftly came under the authority of white Democrats, a period known as the development of the "Solid South." This political realignment reinforced white Democratic supremacy in the South, a tendency that would last for almost a century.

The phrase "Solid South" refers to the near-universal support for the Democratic Party in Southern states, which went uncontested for decades owing to the repression of Black votes and the disenfranchisement of many impoverished whites.

Following the Election of 1872 and the following retreat from Reconstruction, white Democrats in the South moved deliberately to undo the achievements achieved by Black Americans during Reconstruction. Through a mix of legal means, intimidation, and violence, Southern governments established legislation aimed at disenfranchising Black voters.

Poll fees, literacy exams, and the notorious "grandfather clauses" were used to restrict African Americans from voting in elections. These laws were sometimes supported by violent enforcement from organizations like the Klan, which ensured that even those who fit the standards would think twice before trying to vote.

The political supremacy of white Democrats in the South had enormous ramifications for the area and the country. Southern Democrats, commonly nicknamed "Redeemers," aimed to "redeem" the South from Republican authority and restore the social order that had prevailed before the Civil War.

Their actions contributed to the establishment of Jim Crow laws, which formalized racial segregation and inequality. African Americans were forced out of political office, and the South became a bulwark of white supremacy.

Nationally, the Solid South had a huge effect on American politics. For decades, Southern

Democrats had disproportionate authority in Congress, due in part to their largely uncontested election triumphs. This empowered them to affect national policy, frequently in ways that promoted segregation and inequality.

The political partnership between Southern Democrats and their Northern equivalents guaranteed that civil rights issues stayed largely off the national agenda for decades.

The development of the Solid South also heralded the end of the Republican Party's supremacy in the area. While the party had led the country through the Civil War and Reconstruction, its withdrawal from the South in the years after the Election of 1872 enabled Democrats to develop a grip on Southern politics. It would not be until the mid-20th century, during the civil rights struggle, that the political dynamics in the South would begin to alter again.

Chapter 10: Eerie Parallels to Modern Politics

The 1872 election, marred by violence, repression, and a profoundly divided country, seems like a distant episode in American history. However, the circumstances surrounding it bear an uncanny resonance in today's political context. The same fault lines that separated the nation during Reconstruction—racial tensions, voter suppression, political violence, and degradation of democratic norms—continue to resound in the present.

By revisiting this difficult time, we may better grasp how the battles of the past connect to today's issues and how fragile democracy can be when it is not aggressively preserved.

Divided Politics and the Erosion of Democratic Norms

The 1872 election unfolded at a period when the country was strongly divided along racial, political, and geographical lines. The Civil War was concluded, but the scars were still raw. The South, averse to the policies of Reconstruction, was in open revolt against the reforms aimed at integrating emancipated Black residents into political and social life. Political discourse was not a discussion about policy but a war for survival—one that played out brutally in the streets and at the voting box.

Fast-forward to now and the American political environment is equally split. Although the setting has altered, the ideological conflicts remain severe, notably over questions of race, civil rights, and the legitimacy of democratic institutions. The 1872 election was a struggle between two fundamentally opposed factions: one striving for advancement and multiracial democracy, and the other attempting to protect white supremacy and the status quo. In current times, disputes over institutional racism, immigration, and voting rights continue to split the electorate along lines of identity and ideology.

The loss of democratic values in both times is obvious. In 1872, the reluctance of either side to accept the election in Louisiana led to two rival administrations and extensive bloodshed. This hesitation to recognize the validity of an electoral decision recalls recent occurrences in American politics, where the failure to accept election results has led to violent demonstrations and the propagation of disinformation. In both situations, the pillars of democracy—respect for free and fair elections, the peaceful transition of power, and the integrity of institutions—were under threat.

Democracy relies on compromise and the rule of law, but when one side regards its opponents as illegitimate or corrupt, the whole system starts to crumble. The 1872 election highlighted how rapidly a society may descend into turmoil when faith in institutions breaks away.

Today, the loss of democratic norms, from political gerrymandering to efforts to erode faith in election processes, threatens to drag the nation to a similarly deadly brink.

Historical Lessons on Voter Suppression and Political Violence

The 1872 election in Louisiana was characterized by voter suppression and political violence on a vast scale. White supremacist organizations, including the Ku Klux Klan, utilized fear and intimidation to restrict Black votes, destroying polling stations, killing political opponents, and spreading terror across the state.

In Colfax, Louisiana, one of the most terrible acts of political violence occurred when white militias slaughtered over 150 Black men who were protecting their right to vote and participate in the political process. This violence was not simply about winning an election; it was about stopping a multiracial democracy from taking root.

While the brutality of 1872 may seem inconceivable today, voting suppression and political violence are hardly relics of the past. Modern voter suppression takes more subtle but no less destructive forms: restricted voting rules, purges of voter rolls, gerrymandering, and decreased access to polling stations in minority populations.

These measures, however less obviously violent than the acts of terror in 1872, are aimed to accomplish the same goal—undermining the political strength of oppressed people.

Political violence, too, has re-emerged as a tool in today's politicized society. The storming of the U.S. Capitol on January 6, 2021, was a harsh reminder of how fast political violence can develop when driven by disinformation, fear, and a reluctance to accept democratic decisions. Like the armed militias who intimidated Black voters in 1872, current extreme organizations are eager to use force to resist electoral decisions they consider illegitimate.

The lesson from 1872 is clear: voter suppression and political violence are intricately interwoven, and both are aimed at destroying the democratic process. When one group strives to disenfranchise another, it not only erodes the integrity of the election but also raises the possibility of violence, since those who are excluded from the political process are more inclined to perceive it as corrupt and illegitimate.

The Colfax Massacre was not an isolated episode, but part of a bigger trend of using violence to preserve power. Similarly, contemporary political violence and voter suppression are symptoms of a larger ailment in the body politic—one that must be treated if democracy is to survive.

How the 1872 Election Mirrors Today's Political Landscape

The similarities between the election of 1872 and the modern political situation are apparent. Both times are typified by severe polarization, deep-seated racial tensions, and widespread mistrust in institutions. In 1872, the election in Louisiana was considered as a turning moment for the future of Reconstruction and the country's multiracial democracy.

Today, the stakes seem as high, as discussions about voting rights, racial justice, and the validity of elections dominate the political agenda.

In both times, the role of disinformation and media manipulation played a crucial part in stoking divisiveness. In 1872, opposing newspapers stoked the embers of political conflict, publishing fiery language and blatant misinformation about the election and its aftermath. Today, social media has taken on that role, with misinformation operations targeting voters and spreading doubt about the integrity of elections.

The speed and breadth of contemporary technologies have made it simpler than ever to propagate false information, and the ramifications for democracy are serious. When people no longer believe the information they get, it becomes practically difficult to sustain a functioning democracy.

The 1872 election also reflects today in the way political leaders have exploited the divide for personal advantage. In 1872, officials on both sides exploited suspicions of corruption and disloyalty, frequently playing on ethnic tensions to rouse their followers.

Similarly, contemporary political actors have employed aggressive language, fear-mongering, and identity politics to mobilize their followers, sometimes at the price of national unity. This technique has led to greater polarization, making it difficult for the nation to find common ground on crucial issues like voting rights, racial relations, and governance.

Another major resemblance between the two periods is the role of race in affecting political results. In 1872, the election was a war for the future of Black political involvement, with white supremacist organizations doing all in their ability to prevent Black Americans from voting and holding office.

Today, racial tensions continue to impact the political landscape, with arguments over institutional racism, police reform, and immigration policy frequently separating the vote along racial lines. The continuous fight for racial equality in the U.S. serves as a reminder that the war for civil rights and political representation is far from ending.

Perhaps the most troubling resemblance between 1872 and the present is the fragility of democracy itself. The events of 1872 revealed how fast a society may slide into anarchy when the rule of law is neglected, and political violence becomes a weapon of power. Today, the U.S. confronts comparable issues, with democratic values under attack from the inside.

The Capitol rebellion, voter suppression tactics, and escalating political violence all speak to a grave degradation of democratic values—one that, if allowed unchecked, might bring the nation to the edge, just as it did in 1872.

The 1872 election presents a clear warning for today's America. The loss of democratic norms, voter repression, and political violence that marked that time are not merely historical footnotes; they are ongoing challenges that continue to threaten the country's democratic underpinnings. The lessons of 1872 are clear: when a society permits fear, hatred, and intolerance to dictate its politics, democracy itself is in jeopardy.

Chapter 11: What It Takes to Protect Democracy

A multiracial democracy is more than a political system; it is a crucial component of a fair and equitable society. At its essence, it represents a political system where power and representation are inclusive of all racial and ethnic groups. This inclusion is vital for various reasons.

Representation and Equity: A multiracial democracy guarantees that all parts of society have a role in the decision-making process. When different groups are represented, policies are more likely to accommodate the interests and concerns of the whole community, rather than prioritizing a particular racial or ethnic group. This equal representation helps to avoid systematic prejudice and develops a feeling of belonging and involvement among all residents.

Social Stability and Cohesion: Inclusive democracies foster social stability by minimizing the possibility of conflict. When individuals feel that they are adequately represented and that their interests are addressed, they are more likely to contribute constructively to society and less likely to participate in harmful activities. This feeling of inclusion may lessen conflicts between various racial and ethnic groups, leading to a more peaceful society.

Moral and Ethical Imperatives: Beyond practical reasons, a multiracial democracy accords with the moral and ethical ideals of fairness and justice. In a society established on the values of equality, ensuring that all individuals, regardless of color or ethnicity, have equal opportunities and rights is a fundamental obligation. This dedication to diversity represents the underlying ideals upon which democratic societies are formed.

Strength in Diversity: Multiracial democracies benefit from the different ideas and experiences of their people. This variety may lead to more imaginative solutions to social challenges, as varied opinions contribute to a fuller knowledge of complicated situations. Moreover, accepting diversity strengthens a nation's worldwide stature and stimulates international collaboration.

The 1872 election and the difficult era of Reconstruction provide significant lessons for modern leaders attempting to safeguard and develop democracy.

Vigilance Against Corruption and Intimidation: The 1872 election was characterized by extensive corruption, voter intimidation, and bloodshed. Modern leaders must be watchful against these challenges, ensuring that elections are conducted fairly and openly. Effective procedures include tight enforcement of election rules, monitoring for anomalies, and defending the rights of all voters. Leaders should also develop a culture of honesty and accountability throughout political institutions.

The Role of Media and Communication: During the 1872 election, opposing newspapers heightened tensions and fanned bloodshed with sensationalist reporting. In today's digital era, the function of media is even more crucial. Leaders must push for good media and resist disinformation. This requires promoting independent and ethical reporting, teaching the public about media literacy, and tackling the dissemination of misleading information that might undermine democratic processes.

Resolving Racial and Ethnic Conflicts: The violent opposition to Reconstruction and the growth of white supremacist organizations underline the significance of resolving racial and ethnic conflicts. Modern leaders must actively seek to remove structural racism and advocate policies that improve racial justice. This involves adopting anti-discrimination legislation, promoting affirmative action, and developing conversation and understanding across various racial and ethnic populations.

The Importance of Legal Safeguards: The Supreme Court's decision to terminate Reconstruction and the emergence of Jim Crow legislation emphasizes the necessity for comprehensive legal safeguards for civil rights. Leaders must guarantee that legislative frameworks preserve the rights of all people and that any effort to weaken these protections is met with vigorous opposition. This involves defending voting rights, opposing discriminatory practices, and providing equal access to justice.

Building and Maintaining Popular Faith: The instability and bloodshed of 1872 damaged popular faith in the democratic process. Leaders now must seek to regain and retain public confidence by being honest, responsive, and responsible. Engaging with individuals, addressing their problems, and displaying a commitment to democratic values is crucial for developing trust in political institutions.

What the Future Holds if History is Ignored

Ignoring the lessons of history, especially those emphasized by the events of 1872, bears tremendous hazards for the future of democracy.

Erosion of Democratic Norms: If societies overlook the necessity of inclusion and equal representation, democratic norms may weaken. This degradation emerges as diminished political engagement, rising polarization, and the entrenchment of undemocratic behaviors. Without vigilance, the democratic norms that sustain a country may be compromised, resulting in a weaker and less effective political system.

Increased Political Violence and Instability:Failure to address the core causes of political violence and instability might lead to a repeat of similar conflicts. The violent aftermath of the 1872 election serves as a vivid warning of the potential for political conflicts to erupt into widespread bloodshed. Unaddressed complaints, combined with a lack of efficient dispute resolution systems, may lead to greater instability and unrest.

Perpetuation of Inequality and Injustice:Ignoring the need for a multiracial democracy promotes inequality and injustice. Historical injustices that stay ignored may continue to afflict vulnerable populations, leading to continued inequities in opportunities, resources, and rights. This continuation of inequality contradicts the notion of justice and may inhibit social growth.

Weakening of Democratic Institutions: A failure to defend democratic values and safeguard the rights of all people may undermine democratic institutions. Institutions that are not viewed as genuine or fair are less effective and less trusted by the people. This weakening may lead to diminished political involvement and an increasing feeling of disenfranchised among individuals.

Loss of world Influence and Credibility: Democracies that fail to follow their ideals might lose credibility and influence in the world arena. Nations that are viewed as failing to live up to democratic values may risk worldwide censure and lost diplomatic power. This loss of global status might damage a nation's capacity to influence international policy and work on global concerns.

The Cycle of History Repeating Itself: History has a propensity to repeat itself when its lessons are neglected. The events of 1872 indicate how unsolved conflicts may reemerge and lead to more violence. By failing to learn from previous errors, societies risk repeating them, thus endangering their democratic future.

Protecting democracy demands a consistent commitment to diversity, vigilance against corruption and violence, and a determination to learn from the past. By accepting the lessons of the past and working actively to solve contemporary difficulties, leaders may help guarantee that democracy remains healthy and durable. A multiracial democracy, with its principles of justice and representation, is not only a theoretical ideal but a real need for a just and healthy community.

Conclusion

The stormy election of 1872 serves as a vivid reminder of the fragile nature of democracy and the extent to which some would go to subvert it. Through the turmoil, bloodshed, and political upheaval of that age, we witness a vivid mirror of the obstacles encountered in safeguarding democratic norms. As we analyze history, it becomes evident that democracy needs more than simply a viable election system; it involves ongoing attention, dedication, and the active engagement of its population.

The events of 1872 illustrate the deep influence of discriminatory tactics and political violence on the democratic process. The election's violent aftermath and the ensuing growth of segregation and disenfranchisement highlight how fast democratic principles may be destroyed when groups are excluded and when the rule of law is not followed. These historical lessons underline the significance of a multiracial democracy where all voices are heard, and justice is available to everyone.

For current leaders and people alike, the lessons from this tragic chapter of American history are plain. Protecting democracy demands an unshakable commitment to fair and transparent procedures, an aggressive defense against corruption and intimidation, and a solid legal framework that safeguards the rights of all persons.

It necessitates that we face and overcome racial and ethnic divisions with bravery and honesty, establishing a society where every individual has the chance to participate and succeed.

Moreover, the similarities between the divides of 1872 and today's political atmosphere are apparent. The same factors of divisiveness and disenfranchisement that plagued the past are evident in current political fights. As we manage these obstacles, we must heed the lessons of history and strive tirelessly to avoid the repeat of previous errors. Democracy is not a static accomplishment but a living, developing system that demands ongoing care and preservation.

Looking to the future, we must stay diligent in our defense of democratic ideals. The success of our democracy rests on our capacity to learn from the past, to correct contemporary imbalances, and to promote an inclusive society that follows the ideals of justice and equality. By doing so, we remember the hardships and sacrifices of those who came before us and guarantee that democracy remains a vibrant and resilient institution for decades to come.

www.ingramcontent.com/pod-product-compliance
Lightning Source LLC
Chambersburg PA
CBHW071014250726
48653CB00005B/1611